A Note From Rick Renner

I am on a personal quest to see a "revival of the Bible" so people can establish their lives on a firm foundation that will stand strong and endure the test as end-time storm winds begin to intensify.

In order to experience a revival of the Bible in your personal life, it is important to take time each day to read, receive, and apply its truths to your life. James tells us that if we will continue in the perfect law of liberty — refusing to be forgetful hearers, but determined to be doers — we will be blessed in our ways. As you watch or listen to the programs in this series and work through this corresponding study guide, I trust you will search the Scriptures and allow the Holy Spirit to help you hear something new from God's Word that applies specifically to your life. I encourage you to be a doer of the Word He reveals to you. Whatever the cost, I assure you — it will be worth it.

> Thy words were found, and I did eat them;
> and thy word was unto me the joy and rejoicing of mine heart:
> for I am called by thy name, O Lord God of hosts.
> — Jeremiah 15:16

Your brother and friend in Jesus Christ,

Rick Renner

How To Be at Peace With All Men

Copyright © 2021 by Rick Renner
P.O. Box 702040
Tulsa, OK 74170

Published by Rick Renner Ministries
www.renner.org

ISBN 13: 978-1-68031-958-3

eBook ISBN 13: 978-1-68031-959-0

How To Use This Study Guide

This four-lesson study guide corresponds to *"How To Be at Peace With All Men" With Rick Renner* (Renner TV). Each lesson in this study guide covers a topic that is addressed during the program series, with questions and references supplied to draw you deeper into your own private study of the Scriptures on this subject.

To derive the most benefit from this study guide, consider the following:

First, watch or listen to the program prior to working through the corresponding lesson in this guide. (Programs can also be viewed at **renner.org** by clicking on the Media/Archives links.)

Second, take the time to look up the scriptures included in each lesson. Prayerfully consider their application to your own life.

Third, use a journal or notebook to make note of your answers to each lesson's Study Questions and Practical Application challenges.

Fourth, invest specific time in prayer and in the Word of God to consult with the Holy Spirit. Write down the scriptures or insights He reveals to you.

Finally, take action! Whatever the Lord tells you to do according to His Word, do it.

For added insights on this subject, it is recommended that you obtain Rick Renner's books *You Can Get Over It: How To Confront, Forgive, and Move On* and *Sparkling Gems From the Greek, Volumes 1 and 2.* You may also select from Rick's other available resources by placing your order at **renner.org** or by calling 1-800-742-5593.

TOPIC

How To Pursue Peace With All Men

SCRIPTURES

1. **Hebrews 12:14** — Follow peace with all men, and holiness, without which no man shall see the Lord.
2. **1 Corinthians 14:1** — Follow after charity, and desire spiritual gifts, but rather that ye may prophesy.
3. **Romans 14:19** — Let us therefore follow after the things which make for peace, and things wherewith one may edify another.
4. **Romans 12:18** — If it be possible, as much as lieth in you, live peaceably with all men.

GREEK WORDS

1. "follow" — **διώκω** (*dioko*): to follow, to chase, to pursue; a hunting term meaning to deliberately follow after and capture an animal; also translated "persecute"
2. "peace" — **εἰρήνη** (*eirene*): the cessation of war; conflict put away; rebuilding, reconstruction; a time of peace; tranquility
3. "holiness" — **ἁγιασμόν** (*hagiasmon*): from the Greek word (*hagios*) meaning; separate, consecrated, different, holy

SYNOPSIS

The four lessons in this study on *How To Be at Peace With All Men* will focus on the following topics:

- How To Pursue Peace With All Men
- How To Be the Bishop of Your Own Heart
- How To Recognize the Root of Bitterness
- How To Live Free of Offense

The emphasis of this lesson:

How do you obtain peace with a difficult person? Is it even possible to find peace with everyone? To obtain peace we must hunt for it and be deliberate in our pursuit of it. And we must be willing to put aside our weapons of war. We have been set apart to live and respond differently than the world around us and we must do everything within our power to have peace with *all* men.

The Deliberate Pursuit of Peace

We are living in a day of great turmoil and unrest — a time when division and strife between individuals, in cities, and across nations have become commonplace. But in spite of all these things, God has provided a way for us to be at peace with ALL men.

The Bible has much to say about peace and how to obtain it. Hebrews 12:14 says, "Follow peace with all men, and holiness, without which no man shall see the Lord." Notice how this verse begins: "*Follow* after peace...." According to this passage, if we want to obtain peace, we must *follow after it*. But the question is *How?* How do we follow after peace? And what does that mean?

The word "follow" is a translation of the Greek word *dioko*. *Dioko* was commonly used during the First Century and throughout the New Testament as a hunting term. It depicted the acts of a hunter as he *followed, chased, pursued, and hunted* his prey. The *New King James Version* of Hebrews 12:14 says, "*Pursue* peace with all people..." It's interesting that in being instructed to "follow" and *pursue* peace, the Greek word for *hunting* is used. This tells us immediately that if we want to obtain peace in our lives, there are times we must "hunt" for it.

This word *dioko*, translated as "follow," pictures a hunter who dresses in his hunting clothes, grabs his weapons, enters the forest, and hides himself in an attempt to trap the animal that he is hunting. The hunter follows the tracks and scent of the animal while looking for broken branches on bushes and trees that may indicate the direction the animal is moving. He puts forth great effort to pursue and capture his prey.

The writer of Hebrews was saying that this is the kind of determination and attitude we must possess if we are to obtain peace with difficult people in our lives. Like a hunter pursuing his prey, we must follow the scent of peace and the tracks of peace. We need to follow every little clue along the path that will lead to peace.

It must also be noted that hunting is not accidental or haphazard. It is very deliberate and purposeful. If we are to obtain peace with all people, our pursuit must be very deliberate, intentional, and purposeful until we "capture" it.

Persecution Defined

Acts chapter 8 describes a time when the Church was confronted with tremendous persecution. "And Saul was consenting unto his death. And at that time there was a great persecution against the church which was at Jerusalem; and they were all scattered abroad throughout the regions of Judea and Samaria, except the apostles" (Acts 8:1).

Notice it says, "And at that time there was a great *persecution* against the church, which was at Jerusalem." The Greek word for "persecution" here is *dioko*, the very same word used in Hebrews 12:14 translated as "follow."

This verse reveals another aspect of the word *dioko*. Think about this: Is persecution accidental or deliberate? It is deliberate. In the Western world, most people haven't really suffered severe persecution. Persecution, according to the Greek word *dioko*, again, means *to pursue* or *to hunt*. When people are persecuted, someone enacts a plan — a very deliberate and well-executed plan, to determine how to hunt, entrap, or apprehend those individuals.

The instance recounted in Acts 8:1 was persecution against the church in Jerusalem. It wasn't a haphazard event. The religious leaders in Jerusalem actually devised a plan to hunt down Christians and execute them. Often, these religious leaders would disguise themselves as believers. They would find out where the followers of Jesus were gathering and would often follow them to those meetings. These Early New Testament believers were literally *pursued* and *hunted* in the same determined way a hunter pursues his prey.

Following Peace Is Not Spontaneous

Have you ever had a problem with one of your relatives, a co-worker, or a friend? Maybe you've had an issue with someone at church and it seems every time you're around that person there is friction and tension.

Following after peace cannot be something you do spontaneously. To be at peace with the people in your life, you must have a plan and be determined to pursue it.

The next time you know you will be with that person, pray and allow the Holy Spirit to give you a plan. He knows the key to *every* person's heart. He knows how to resolve *every* conflict. If you will take time to listen to the Holy Spirit, He will fill your mouth with what to say and what not to say. He will tell you how to act and how not to act. The Holy Spirit knows exactly what you need to do if you will simply make it a matter of prayer. He will give you a plan which you can then very deliberately follow — *dioko* — to have peace with all men.

There are two more examples of the word "follow," translated from the Greek word *dioko*. The first is found in First Corinthians 14:1 which says, "Follow after charity, and desire spiritual gifts, but rather that ye may prophesy." It's interesting to note that in the *King James Version*, the Apostle Paul's words were translated, "Follow after *charity...*" The original Greek says, "Follow after *love.*"

The word "follow" is once again the Greek word *dioko*, the hunting term. In essence, Paul was saying in First Corinthians 14:1, if you want love, you must *dioko — follow after it*. You cannot wait for it to come to you. If you want loving relationships, you must put on your "hunting gear" and make a decision and say, "I'm not going to wait for love to come walking in my direction. I'm going to go after love. I'm going to do everything within my power to capture love. I'm going to execute a plan and pursue it until I have obtained loving relationships."

A second example is found in Romans 14 which says, "Let us therefore follow after the things which make for peace, and things wherewith one may edify another" (Romans 14:19). The phrase "follow after" is, again, translated from the Greek word *dioko*, but in this instance it is a participle, which means this is something we are to do *habitually*. Following after peace needs to be our pattern; our way of living; our lifestyle. We are to *habitually* and *consistently* follow after peace.

Put Away the Weapons of War

Romans 14:19 continues, "...follow after the things which make for *peace...*." The word "peace" in this verse is the Greek word *eirene*, and it describes *the cessation of war*. It denotes *tranquility; the euphoric feelings of gratification, relaxation, and peace that follow a time of war.* Where hostility once existed, the weapons of war have been put away. Where all human effort was invested in fighting and conflict, it has ceased and it is now a period of rebuilding and reconstruction.

This word *eirene* is often translated as "tranquility." When Romans 14:19 says, "...follow after the things which make for peace," it is an inspired command to put away our weapons so we may have peace or tranquility in our relationships rather than using our energies for fighting and conflict.

The word "things" is the Greek word *ta*, and in Romans 14:19 it means *embracing anything that makes for peace.* These "things" may include admitting you were wrong about something or asking for forgiveness. It may mean taking the high road even if the other person was the offender. It means doing *whatever we must do to pursue peace*, to obtain it, and begin the process of rebuilding and reconstructing the relationship.

If It Is Possible

Looking again at Hebrews 12:14, it says we are to pursue peace with *"all"* men." You may be thinking to yourself, *Is it even possible to have peace with "all" men?* Romans 12:18 answers that question: "If it be possible, as much as lieth in you, live peaceably with all men."

The word "possible" in this verse is from the Greek word *dunatos*, which means *feasible, doable, or achievable.* Notice, Romans 12:18 begins with the word "if," which implies there are times when it is *not* feasible. The Greek word *dunatos*, translated "possible," implies that great effort and concentration will be necessary. It indicates something is going to be very difficult to achieve, but in most cases, it is achievable.

Notice again, Hebrews 12:14 states, "Follow peace with all men..." It does not say "with *some* men" or "with *a few* men." It says "ALL men," indicating this is God's will and desire. It may not always be easy, but it is definitely something we need to pursue with determination.

Set Apart

Continuing with Hebrews 12:14: "Follow peace with all men, and holiness, without which no man shall see the Lord." The word for "holiness" is the Greek word *hagiasmon*, which means *something that is separate or something that is different.* The Bible is called the *Holy* Bible. It is in a different category than any other book — it is *holy, separate, unique, sanctified, and set apart.*

In the Old Testament, particularly in the book of Exodus, when the presence of God touched the mountain, it became "holy" — the Greek word *hagios* — *separated* or *set apart* from all the other mountains. Even though it was surrounded by many other mountains, this mountain was different from all the others because the presence of God had touched it.

Likewise, the New Testament called believers "saints" (*see* 2 Corinthians 13:13; Ephesians 3:18 and 6:18; Romans 12:13 and 15:25; and Philippians 4:21-22), which was also translated from the Greek word *hagios.* The word "saint" means *holy.* And as "saints" in Jesus Christ, we are called to be *different, unique,* and *separated.* The blood of Jesus Christ touched us, the Holy Spirit came into our life, and the presence of God came upon us when we were born again.

Just as the presence of God sanctified the Bible and set it apart, and as the presence of God sanctified the mountain and set it apart from the other mountains, when the blood of Jesus touched our lives and the Holy Spirit came into us, we were set apart. We may look like other people, but we are *not* like other people. Our behavior should not be the same as that of the world. All of those works of God have sanctified us, and we are *separated* from the rest of the world — He made us to be *different.*

A person who is not sanctified may respond by arguing when confronted with an argumentative person. That is how the world typically behaves. But for a believer there is a higher standard. We are to behave like "holy" people — we are different.

Blocked From the Presence of the Lord

Hebrews 12:14 concludes, "... without which no man *shall see* the Lord." One expositor describes the words "shall see" as meaning "without which no man will be admitted into the presence of the Lord *right now.*" In other words, strife, bad relationships, or hostile feelings will block us from experiencing the presence of the Lord in our lives *right now,* at this *current moment.*

Imagine you have hostility in your heart toward a family member. You go to church and you feel nothing of God's presence even though you are surrounded by people worshiping the Lord and experiencing His presence.

When you pray, it feels like those prayers are going no further than the ceiling.

The Holy Spirit lives in believers (*see* John 14:16) but the fact that He lives in us doesn't mean we always feel or enjoy His presence. When we have strife or anger in our hearts, it prohibits us from entering the enjoyable presence of the Lord.

Rick recounted a situation when he struggled in this area:

> Decades ago, when Denise and I first moved to the Soviet Union, God was blessing our ministry. But there was a pastor in town that I wasn't fond of because I disagreed with his doctrine. I didn't like him, and he didn't like me. I was immature at the time and wrongly said some negative things about him publicly. Things escalated between us, but I kept justifying my behavior. I believed this pastor was wrong and I was right, and I took it upon myself to rectify the situation. I believed I was the one who was supposed to 'handle it,' but my attitude was terrible, and I was blind to it.
>
> One day while I was praying, the Lord asked me, 'Rick, do you want revival in your life?' And of course I responded, 'Lord, you know that I do.'
>
> He asked me a second time, 'Rick, do you really want revival in your life?' And I answered, 'Lord, I've already answered You. Yes, I want revival in my life.'
>
> He asked me the same question a third time. I said, 'Yes, Lord, I *really* want revival in my life.' And He responded, 'If you want revival, I want you to go to that pastor, get on your knees in front of him, and ask for forgiveness for your attitude.'
>
> I immediately answered, 'And what about *his* attitude? What about *him*?' And the Holy Spirit said, 'I'm not talking to you about him, I'm talking to you about *you*. If you are going to have revival, you need to put some of these attitudes permanently to rest. I'm not talking to you about him and what he needs to do, I'm telling you to go to him, get on your knees, and ask for forgiveness.'
>
> I considered this man to be arrogant and prideful, and the thought of getting on my knees in front of him I knew would just

thrill this pastor. To be honest, I did not immediately obey the Lord. I argued with Him for several weeks.

Finally, the day came when I said, 'Okay Lord, I want revival. I want to be free! I want Your presence. I want to know Your power in my life and in my church. I am going to him now. I'm going to obey You.'

The Lord helped me to do the things that were necessary to obtain peace, and to this day that man is a precious friend of mine. After I obeyed the Lord, revival came to our church.

It was me and my bad attitude that had been blocking revival all along.

Strife, conflict, and rage in our hearts can block us from experiencing God's presence. According to Hebrews 12:14, we must follow after peace and holiness. God expects believers to take the high road. We must be consecrated in our attitudes and actions and do whatever is necessary to "capture" peace with all men so we may experience the presence of the Lord in our lives, then carry that presence to the world.

STUDY QUESTIONS

Study to shew thyself approved unto God, a workman that needeth not to be ashamed, rightly dividing the word of truth.
— 2 Timothy 2:15

1. What specific instruction is given to us in Hebrews 12:14? Share three other scripture passages that underscore this same truth.
2. Provide an example that describes what it looks like to "seek and pursue peace with all men."
3. What can happen to our relationship with God if we do not pursue peace with others?

PRACTICAL APPLICATION

But be ye doers of the word, and not hearers only, deceiving your own selves.
— James 1:22

1. Can you identify some hindrances in your own life, either past or current, that are or have contributed to difficulty between you and certain people?

2. What did you do or must you do currently to pursue and capture peace between you and them? Ask the Holy Spirit to help you.

3. List ways you can personally keep yourself from being blocked from the presence of the Lord.

TOPIC

How To Be the Bishop of Your Own Heart

SCRIPTURES

1. **Hebrews 12:14** — Follow peace with all men, and holiness, without which no man shall see the Lord.

2. **1 Corinthians 14:1** — Follow after charity, and desire spiritual gifts, but rather that ye may prophesy.

3. **Hebrews 12:15** — Looking diligently lest any man fail of the grace of God; lest any root of bitterness springing up trouble you, and thereby many be defiled.

4. **2 Corinthians 6:1** — We then, as workers together with him, beseech you also that ye receive not the grace of God in vain.

5. **Galatians 2:21** — I do not frustrate the grace of God: for if righteousness come by the law, then Christ is dead in vain.

GREEK WORDS

1. "follow" — διώκω (*dioko*): a hunting term: to follow, to chase, to pursue, to hunt

2. "peace" — εἰρήνη (*eirene*): the cessation of war, conflict put away, rebuilding, reconstruction, a time of peace; tranquility

3. "holiness" — ἅγιος (*hagiasmon*): from the Greek word (*hagios*) meaning; separate, consecrated, different, holy

4. "looking diligently"— ἐπισκοπέω (*episkopeo*): a compound of ἐπι (*epi*) and σκοπέω (*skopeo*);

5. the prefix (*epi*) means over; and the verb (*skopeo*) means to look; compounded, *episkopeo* means to look over something; pictures oversight; depicts someone in a supervisory position; bishop

6. "grace"— χάρις (*charis*): an empowering touch that transforms

7. "root"— ῥίζα (*ridza*): something deeply rooted; fixed into place

8. "bitterness"— πικρία (*pichria*): caustic, sour, sharp, or bitter; denotes an inward attitude that is so bitter, it produces a scowl on one's face

SYNOPSIS

In our last lesson we studied what it means to *follow after peace* in our daily lives. Hebrews 12:14, our foundational text, says, "Follow peace with all men, and holiness, without which no man shall see the Lord."

We learned the Greek word for "follow" is *dioko*, which originally described a hunter who put on his hunting gear and grabbed his weapons to capture an animal. He would follow the scent and tracks of that animal he was hunting and would even look for broken branches indicating the hunted animal's path. The hunter would follow aggressively and consistently until the hunted game was captured and bagged. Hunting was done purposefully and it was planned out in advance. Like a hunter, we are to *pursue* "peace with all men."

Hebrews 12:14 continues, "Follow *peace* with all men." The word "peace" in this verse is the Greek word *eirene*, and it describes *the cessation of war*. It denotes *tranquility; the euphoric feelings of gratification, relaxation, and peace that follow a time of war*. If we want to have "peace with all men," sometimes we must hunt for it, and there are times when it can be hard to find.

We also studied Acts 8:1, which states, "…At that time there was a great persecution against the church which was at Jerusalem…." We learned the Greek word for "persecution" is also *dioko* — the same word translated "follow" in Hebrews 12:14 — and carries the idea of premeditated thought. Whether someone is following after peace or persecuting someone, it is not accidental — it is very deliberate. To "follow" peace means we are to hunt for it. Even when it's hard to find with difficult people, we must follow every clue to "capture" peace with all men.

In First Corinthians 14:1, again we are told to "follow" after love — the same Greek word *dioko*. If we want loving relationships, we cannot wait for them to come our way. We must put on our "hunting gear" until we finally "capture" loving relationships in our lives.

In addition, we learned that not only are we to follow peace with all men, but we are also to follow "holiness," translated from the Greek word *hagiasmon*. Hebrews 12:14 exhorts us: "Follow peace with all men, and holiness (*hagiasmon*), without which no man shall see the Lord." God wants us to put away the fighting and conflict to enter a time of peace and reconstruction (*see* Romans 14:19). If we have strife, conflict, hostility or raging in our hearts, it will block us from experiencing the presence of God here on earth.

The emphasis of this lesson:

You are the bishop of your own heart. But if you allow bitterness to take root in your heart, it's possible for the grace of God to be ineffective in your life. Thankfully, you can learn to recognize bitterness and pull it out from its roots.

You Are the Bishop of Your Own Heart

How are we to put away those attitudes that block us from God's presence? How do we deal with strife, unforgiveness, and offense? Hebrews 12:15 gives us insight to these questions: "Looking diligently lest any man fail of the grace of God; lest any root of bitterness springing up trouble you, and thereby many be defiled."

The Greek word for "looking diligently" is *episkopeo*. It is a compound of the two Greek words *epi*, which means *over*, and *skopeo*, which means *to look*. The word *skopeo* is where we get the term *microscope*. When the word *skopeo* is compounded with the word *epi* to form *episkopeo*, it means *to look over*, *to look over something*. It also means *oversight, administration*; *being in management or having a supervisory position*.

The word *episkopeo* is also found in First Timothy 3 where the Apostle Paul describes the qualifications required for someone to hold the position of a "bishop" in the church. "...If a man desire the office of a bishop, he desireth a good work" (1 Timothy 3:1). The word "bishop" is a translation from the same Greek word *episkopeo*. This individual has a *supervisory position* and will be held accountable for what happens in the churches he manages and oversees. If the churches he stewards prosper and do well, he will probably receive credit for it. But if those churches do poorly or fail, he will likely receive the blame.

Looking again at Hebrews 12:15, the verse begins with the same Greek word *episkopeo*, translated here as "looking diligently." The writer of Hebrews is telling you and me that we are bishops. All who know Jesus are bishops. But what are we bishops over? Every born-again believer is a bishop over his or her own heart. Your heart is completely under your care, management, and supervision, and God will ultimately hold you responsible for the condition of your own heart.

You cannot blame someone else for offense, strife, hatred or bitterness you hold in your own heart. You cannot blame your family history, your spouse, friend or neighbor for what you harbor in your heart. You are a child of God and are now responsible for the condition of your own heart. You are the bishop — the *overseer* — of your heart.

If you are in a difficult relationship and tend to be offended by it, the offense is your fault. Maybe the other person was really in the wrong, but you alone have the authority to say "yes" to holding an offense. Only you can give entrance to unforgiveness. We must depend on the Holy Spirit to learn how to walk free of those things that keep us from being able to draw near to God.

Do Not Fail of the Grace of God

Hebrews 12:15 continues, "Looking diligently lest any man fail of the grace of God." The phrase "fail of the grace of God" is rather a strange verse. The grace of God is free — we don't earn it or deserve it, so how could we possibly *fail* at it? Yet the verse clearly states that we can "fail the grace of God."

And Second Corinthians 6:1 says something very similar: "We then, as workers together with Him beseech you also that ye receive not the grace of God in vain." The word "vain" here is a translation of the Greek word *kenos*, which describes something *fruitless* or *wasted; something that has no effect*. God's grace doesn't always have an effect, even when it comes to us. We can receive the grace of God *in vain*.

Furthermore, the Apostle Paul states that it is possible to *frustrate* the grace of God when he declared, "I do not frustrate the grace of God: for if righteousness comes by the law, then Christ is dead in vain" (Galatians 2:21). Here we see a picture of the grace of God coming to an individual. When we tap into the grace of God, it *always* empowers us to *do* something.

The word "grace" is the Greek word *charis*. This word was used in the New Testament to describe an individual who was a pagan and was considered to be *graced by the gods* or *touched supernaturally*. For the believer, a person graced by God receives a supernatural touch from God that empowers that person to do what he or she could never do naturally. It is an empowering touch that changes us, changes our attitudes — it *transforms* us. When the grace of God touches our life we are suddenly enabled to think and behave differently. The important thing about grace is that we can either accept or reject it.

Imagine an individual who has unforgiveness in his heart toward his spouse. They are together in a worship service and the grace of God comes on him and he is flooded with thoughts of forgiveness toward his spouse. Suddenly, God is empowering him to make things right between him and his wife, but instead of acting on it, he says in his heart "No, I'm not doing that. I am unwilling to forgive her." This man has just rejected the grace of God and that grace is in vain — it is futile, wasted, and unable to fulfill the purpose for which God sent it.

The grace of God is powerful and has the ability to do what it was sent to do, but there must be a recipient who will cooperate with that grace. If we don't cooperate with God's grace, we can frustrate it, receive it in vain, or fail of it. Don't fail, frustrate, or reject the grace of God. You are the bishop of your own heart, and if you refuse to deal with your heart, Hebrews 12:15 tells us that a root of bitterness can spring up and affect many.

The Root of Bitterness

Hebrews 12:15 concludes, "...lest any man fail of the grace of God; lest any *root* of *bitterness* springing up trouble you, and thereby many be defiled." The word "root" is the Greek word *ridza*, which describes *something deeply rooted* or *fixed into place*. Bitterness has a way of sending tentacles into the soil of our hearts, the soil of our emotions, and the soil of our soul. The tentacles can be so far-reaching they can even pass from one generation to the next. They can be passed to an entire nation!

The word "bitterness" is the Greek word *pichria*, and it denotes *an inward attitude that is so bitter, it produces a scowl on one's face*. It describes someone who is caustic, sour, or sharp; one who has become so inwardly infected with bitterness that it affects their outward appearance or attitude. What is in your heart will eventually reveal itself. If you are bitter, it will be evident in your expressions and your words. Jesus said clearly that "out of the abundance of the heart his mouth speaks" (Luke 6:45 *NKJV*). Whatever we fill our hearts with, our mouths will speak.

I challenge you to pay attention to what you're saying to your spouse, family, or friends. Do you take every opportunity to sneak in a little negativity about someone? If you do, it's a sign that you need to check your heart for a bitter root that's beginning to produce fruit. Beware — it's poisonous for you, and poisonous for those who eat of it. The good news is that it's a simple act of repentance that rips out the roots of bitterness from your heart. It causes the Holy Spirit to dive deep into the recesses of the heart to tear out those bitter roots so you can walk free!

STUDY QUESTIONS

> Study to shew thyself approved unto God, a workman that needeth
> not to be ashamed, rightly dividing the word of truth.
> — 2 Timothy 2:15

1. What does it mean to be "the bishop over your own heart"?
2. Explain what it means to "fail of the grace of God" according to Hebrews 12:15. Provide two scriptural examples.
3. What is the function of grace in the life of a believer?
4. Describe the root of bitterness and its source.

PRACTICAL APPLICATION

> But be ye doers of the word, and not hearers only,
> deceiving your own selves.
> — James 1:22

1. Think of a time when you harbored unforgiveness in your heart toward someone who offended you. Explain how this relates to being the *bishop* of your own heart.

2. Relate a time when you frustrated the grace of God in your life. What adjustments did you make to cooperate with the grace of God in this particular instance?

3. Take a day and pay attention to what you are saying to those closest to you. Examine your heart, and if there is any bitter root springing up in your heart, pull it out through repentance.

LESSON 3

TOPIC

How To Recognize the Root of Bitterness

SCRIPTURES

1. **Hebrews 12:14** — Follow peace with all men, and holiness, without which no man shall see the Lord.

2. **Hebrews 12:15** — Looking diligently lest any man fail of the grace of God; lest any root of bitterness springing up trouble you, and thereby many be defiled.

3. **2 Corinthians 6:1** — We then, as workers together with him, beseech you also that ye receive not the grace of God in vain.

GREEK WORDS

1. "looking diligently"— ἐπισκοπέω (*episkopeo*): a compound of ἐπι (*epi*) and σκοπέω (*skopeo*); the prefix (*epi*) means over; and the verb (*skopeo*) means to look; compounded, *episkopeo* means to look over something; pictures oversight; depicts someone in a supervisory position; bishop

2. "grace" — χάρις (*charis*): an empowering touch that enables you to do what you could never do by yourself

3. "root"— ῥίζα (*ridza*): a root system that is very deep

4. "springing up" — φύω (*phuo*): a small plant that pierces its way through the soil

5. "trouble" — ἐνοχλέω (*enochleo*): harassed, hounded, troubled; denotes something that bothers and upsets someone; pictures a stalker

SYNOPSIS

The message from our last lesson is so important that I want to focus again on what we taught so it penetrates deep into your heart and transforms your thinking and your life.

Hebrews 12:15 says, "Looking diligently lest any man fail of the grace of God; lest any root of bitterness springing up trouble you and thereby many be defiled." The Greek word for "looking diligently" is *episkopeo* and it carries the idea of *a person entrusted with managerial responsibilities*. It denotes *someone who has oversight, administrates or manages*. It is also the same Greek word that is translated "bishop" in First Timothy 3:1.

If things go well in the area over which the manager has oversight, he will receive the credit. But if things go poorly, he will also receive the blame. This passage tells us that we have the oversight of our own heart — we alone are responsible for the inner condition of our heart. We cannot blame others for its condition, and what happens in our heart can only happen with our permission.

Hebrews 12:15 continues, "Looking diligently lest any man fail of the grace of God." If we do not take responsibility for the condition of our own hearts, we can "fail of the grace of God." And as we studied in our last lesson, the Greek word for "grace" is *charis*, and describes *an empowering touch from God that enables us to do what we normally could never do by ourselves.*

The emphasis of this lesson:

The root of bitterness is a result of wasting the grace of God that has been provided for us. In this lesson you will learn how to recognize the root of bitterness and how to remove it from your life so you can live permanently free of it.

The Root of Bitterness Reexamined

Continuing with Hebrews 12:15: "Looking diligently lest any man fail of the grace of God...." The word "fail" here is the Greek word *husteros*, which means *to be left in a place of deficiency* or *to be behind*. If we reject God's grace, we will *fail of it* (see Hebrews 12:15), *frustrate it* (see Galatians 2:21), or receive it *in vain* (see 2 Corinthians 6:1), and that grace will be *futile* and *wasted*. When grace is made available to us by God, that grace has come to help us do what we couldn't do on our own. But if we reject it, we are left with only our own strength.

The result of this deficit is found in the second half of Hebrews 12:15: "…lest any root of bitterness springing up trouble you, and thereby many be defiled." As we discussed previously, by rejecting the grace of God, a root of bitterness can spring up in our heart. The Greek word *ridza*, translated "root," describes *a very, very deep root system.* Bitterness may begin as something very small, but if it's allowed to fester it will send deep tentacles into your heart and become deeply rooted into your emotions.

The Greek word for "bitterness" is *pichria*, which describes *something horribly bitter, tart, or sharp.* It carries the idea of *something that is caustic.* A person with bitterness in their heart is very cynical and skeptical, is often unpleasant to be around, and seems to verbally assault everything and everyone.

And the phrase "springing up" is the Greek word *phuo* and describes *a little plant just beginning to pierce its way through the soil.* Rick recalled a memory from his childhood that came to mind from the words "springing up." He said, "I remember when I was a boy, I loved to plant things in our backyard. After planting seeds, every day I would look in the yard to see if anything was growing. After waiting and waiting, I would get so excited when I would see a little shoot pierce its way up through the soil. That small shoot was evidence that the seed I had planted was working!"

When the root of bitterness has been sown in your heart, you will know it because the evidence of it will begin to pierce its way up to the surface. Bitterness never stays silent or hidden; it always shows up.

How To Recognize Bitterness

There are a number of ways bitterness begins to manifest in our lives, but let's look at the two most common ways. First, bitterness manifests in our thinking. It distorts our thoughts and causes us to think negatively about any given situation. Next, it shows up in our words by what comes out of our mouth. If we want to know what's in a person's heart, listen to what's coming out of their mouth. Jesus admonished, "…For out of the abundance of the heart his mouth speaks" (Luke 6:45 *NKJV*). The mouth is the revealer of the heart. People will talk about what they love. But if they're upset about something you will know it because it will be revealed in the words they speak. If they're at peace in their heart, they will speak peace-filled words. The mouth is ALWAYS the revealer of the heart — ALWAYS.

Again, I challenge you to pay attention to what's coming out of your mouth. When you hear yourself saying things not worthy of your mouth, it's time for you to go to the Lord and repent. By asking for forgiveness, you rip the tentacles of bitterness from your heart.

Hounded by Bitterness

The second half of Hebrews 12:15 continues, "…lest a root of bitterness springing up trouble you." In Greek, the word "trouble" is *enochleo*, and it means more than to just be troubled. *Enochleo* — the word translated as "troubled" — describes *a person who is harassed and hounded by his thoughts*. One expositor describes *enochleo* as a picture of a stalker. Bitterness will show up in your mouth and begin to dominate your mind and emotions; it hounds you.

At times, someone who has offended us doesn't even realize they have done so. Think of moments when you discovered you had offended someone. Did you offend them on purpose? More than likely, no. Often, we are shocked to learn how the offended person wrongly perceived our words or actions.

Maybe a co-worker is preoccupied in their mind about something and passes you in the hallway and completely ignores you without even realizing it. You become offended, perceiving that they have rejected you. You take offense and become harassed with thoughts about them ignoring you. *Why did they ignore me? What have I ever done to them to deserve this? Why did they do this? Why did they not do this? Why did they say that? Why did they not say that?*

The thoughts of this incident can begin to hound, harass, and stalk you. You think about them when you go to bed. You think about them when you wake up. Anytime there is a silent pause in your day, thoughts of that person fill your mind. This demonstrates what "trouble" means in verse 15.

Don't Make a Stain

Again, Hebrews 12:15 says, "Looking diligently lest any man fail of the grace of God; lest any root of bitterness springing up trouble you, and thereby many be defiled." The words "be defiled" is a translation of the Greek word *miaino*, meaning *to stain* or *to spot*.

Imagine you are visiting a friend who has white carpet in their home. As you walk across the room carrying a glass of grape juice, you trip and drop the entire glass of juice on the white carpet. The carpet becomes stained with the purple grape juice. We could say this juice has "defiled" the carpet. Because it's grape juice, it is very difficult to remove the stain. You may scrub and scrub and scrub the carpet, but the stain remains. Even if your friend forgives you for dropping the juice, every time they pass that stain, they're going to remember you. That stain is a permanent reminder of something that happened in the past. This illustrates the idea behind the word *miaino* — translated "to be defiled."

A person who has a root of bitterness eventually reveals that bitterness by the words they speak to the people around them. Those people around a bitter person are like that white carpet. Bitter words *stain* them. By allowing bitter words to come from your mouth, you are defiling and staining the people who are hearing those words. You are spotting them with ugly, insensitive, and unkind words and with tainted opinions. And you are leaving a permanent stain in the ears of the listeners.

Let's say there's a man who got saved in a particular church. His life was changed and he loves the church. He's a huge fan of the pastor and his preaching, and he is submitted to the authority of the pastor. He brings his family to the church and they worship together. And when they are at home they talk enthusiastically about the church and their pastor. They're so grateful. But one day, the pastor does something that disappoints this man. Remember, pastors are human and sometimes they disappoint us. But this man becomes offended.

Rather than taking that offense to the Lord, this husband and father allows the offense to grow inside his heart. Now, instead of sitting around the dinner table and talking about how wonderful the church is and how much he loves the pastor, the offense begins to manifest in his mouth. He complains, "Well, I just don't enjoy church like I used to. I think maybe the church really isn't what we thought it was."

As the offense begins to show up in this father's mouth, his wife and children are listening to those words. Until this moment, his children loved the church as they should; they loved the pastor and looked forward to being in the church.

But this man begins to spew the offense in his heart and defile many, including his own wife and children. This man "stains" his family with his offense. Now his wife and children don't want to go to church because, in their thinking, the church is filled with hypocrites. They no longer want to hear the pastor teach the Word of God because they now believe he isn't really who he says he is.

However, one day this man gets his heart right with God, repents, and goes to the pastor and asks for forgiveness. Unfortunately, his kids now have a problem. *He* is free but his wife and kids are now bitter toward the church.

Think about how many times you have been affected by what someone has told you about another person. Now every time you see that person, you think about what you heard about them. What happened? You became defiled. You became spotted. Your thoughts became stained by the words of another person.

Our words either help or hurt, so we need to take responsibility for our mouths. What are you saying that negatively affects your kids, your friends, and the relationships of those around you? What kind of *stain* are you leaving in their ears? Or are you, instead, speaking grace to those who are listening to you?

If there is a root of bitterness in your heart and it's beginning to produce negative fruit, I encourage you to humble yourself before the Lord, repent, and rip that root of bitterness out of your heart. Then your mouth will be filled with grace and bring life and encouragement to those around you.

STUDY QUESTIONS

Study to shew thyself approved unto God, a workman that needeth not to be ashamed, rightly dividing the word of truth.
— 2 Timothy 2:15

1. What is the main indicator that we may have a root of bitterness?
2. Describe the meaning of the Greek word *miaino* and how it can affect the people around you.

PRACTICAL APPLICATION

But be ye doers of the word, and not hearers only,
deceiving your own selves.
— James 1:22

1. Have you been deeply hurt by someone and cannot seem to let go of the offense? Is bitterness stalking you? If so, according to Colossians 3:13, what do you need to do?

2. Are you anchored to an offense from the past in a way that threatens to sabotage your future? Take time with the Holy Spirit who is your Counselor and ask Him to reveal to you the root of your offense. Surrender that wounded place to Him as you forgive.

LESSON 4

TOPIC

How To Live Free of Offense

SCRIPTURES

1. **Luke 17:1** — Then said he unto the disciples, It is impossible but that offences will come: but woe unto him, through whom they come!

2. **Luke 17:3** — Take heed to yourselves: If thy brother trespass against thee, rebuke him; and if he repent, forgive him.

3. **Luke 17:4** — And if he trespass against thee seven times in a day, and seven times in a day turn again to thee, saying, I repent; thou shall forgive him.

4. **Luke 17:5** — And the apostles said unto the Lord, Increase our faith.

5. **Luke 17:6** — And the Lord said, If ye had faith as a grain of mustard seed, ye might say unto this sycamine tree, Be thou plucked up by the root, and be thou planted in the sea; and it should obey you.

6. **Hebrews 12:15** — Looking diligently lest any man fail of the grace of God; lest any root of bitterness springing up trouble you, and thereby many be defiled.

GREEK WORDS

1. "offense" — **σκάνδαλον** (*skandalon*): scandalous, a term used to describe the trapping of an animal; entrapment
2. "forgive" — **ἀφίημι** (*aphiemi*): to forgive, disregard, let it go; to permanently dismiss; to release

SYNOPSIS

There is nothing worse than being offended. When you are offended, it hounds you, stalks you, harasses you, and affects your entire quality of life. But if you *are* offended, there is a way for you to get offense out of your life so you can be free of it. In Luke 17, we will discover how we can deal with offenses when they present themselves in our lives.

The emphasis of this lesson:

It is easy to be entrapped by offense, but Jesus gives us clear instructions about how to live free of it. We can speak to offense in our lives and it requires only mustard seed faith. We have the ability to destroy the roots of offense and walk in the freedom Jesus promises.

Don't Be Entrapped by Offense

Jesus states in Luke 17:1, "…It is impossible but that offences will come: but woe unto him, through whom they come!" In this scripture, Jesus is basically telling us, "If you live in this world and deal with people, at some point you will have an opportunity to be offended." The possibility of offense comes to everyone.

What is an "offense"? The word "offense" comes from the Greek word *skandalon* which is where we get the word "scandal." It means *scandalous*, and it was also *a term used to describe the entrapment of an animal.*

The word *skandalon,* translated here as "offense," originally described the small piece of wood that was used to keep the door of an animal trap propped open. A piece of food was placed in the trap to lure the animal inside. When the animal entered the trap and accidentally bumped the *skandalon*, or the small piece of wood, the *skandalon* collapsed, causing the door of the trap to slam shut and the animal to be caught inside with no way to escape.

An offense has the potential to entrap us in our mind and emotions. Jesus used this word to warn us about events that happen in our life that carry the potential to trip us up. When we become offended, it is a *scandal* in our mind and in our emotions. The offense traps us and holds us captive.

Two Reasons for Offense

Every form of offense will fall into one of these two categories:

1. Because of what someone did or said.
2. Because of what someone did *not* do or did *not* say.

When you are offended there is a scandal or process of entrapment attempting to take place in your mind. Maybe someone did something different than you expected or they said something below your expectation of them and it caused offense and disappointment in your soul.

Or perhaps you were walking through a difficult season in your life and you expected someone would call, text, send a note of encouragement, or bring a meal. But instead, that person did absolutely nothing, and because of his or her omission, you became offended. We become offended because of *acts of commission* — something offensive someone did or said to us — or *acts of omission* — something someone did *not* say or did *not* do.

In Luke 17, Jesus was admonishing the disciples concerning offense, and it applies to us today — it is impossible to live this life without the possibility of being offended, so we must learn to deal with offense correctly.

Get a Grip

Jesus continued his warning to the disciples saying, "Take heed to yourselves: If thy brother trespass against thee, rebuke him, and if he repent, forgive him" (Luke 17:3). Often when we are offended by someone we want to confront them. But Jesus said we are to "take *heed* to yourself."

The word "heed" here is the Greek word *epecho*, which is a compound of the words *ep* and *echo*. The word *ep* means *on*, and the word *echo* means *to have* or *to hold*. Compounded, *epecho* — translated here as "heed"— means *to grab hold of something very tightly.* It pictures *getting a grip on yourself.*

"*Getting a grip*" doesn't mean doing whatever you want to do when you are offended. You may literally want to "get a grip" on the person who offended you. You may want to point out what they have done and how hurtful they have been. But Jesus said, "Wait, wait, wait! Before you go to that person, before you take any action, stop and *take heed to yourself.*"

Before confronting the one who has offended you — get a grip on yourself. Pause and ask yourself some important questions: *Did that individual really intend to offend me? Did they have a plot to entrap me in offense?* Put aside your emotions and pray before you make the decision to confront them. Give yourself time for the anger and disappointment to subside. Pause before rushing into action.

Rick recounted, "In my own life, I have learned that if I'm in a difficult conversation and I am tempted to be offended, sometimes it is best for me to excuse myself for about 10 or 15 minutes." If you are being confronted with offense and it is at all possible, go for a brief walk or close your eyes for a few minutes or even go into another room and pray. Pray in tongues. Get into a place of peace. Then, when you have taken a moment to put your emotions aside, you can return to that conversation calmly.

What Does It Mean To "Rebuke"?

Luke 17:3 continues, "…If thy brother trespass against thee, rebuke him…." The meaning of "trespass" here means *to cross a line* or *to violate*. If you feel that someone has crossed a line inappropriately, if someone has transgressed, said something they shouldn't have said, touched something they shouldn't have touched, gone somewhere they shouldn't have gone, Jesus tells us it is okay to go to that person.

If someone has "trespassed" against you, the word says to "rebuke" them. "Rebuke" sounds very dramatic, but in this context, it means *to talk about it* or *confront them.* There is a kind way to confront or have a conversation with someone who has crossed a line.

He said, "rebuke" them. Approach that person with reconciliation in your heart rather than accusation. Spiritual maturity and responsibility are important in bringing rebuke to someone who has crossed a line or violated us in some area of our lives.

Repentance and Forgiveness

Luke 17:3 concludes, "…And if he *repent, forgive* him." The Greek word for "repent" in this verse is *metanoeo,* and it means *to change one's mind.* It pictures *a change of mind that results in a complete, radical, total change of behavior.* And it denotes *a decision to completely change or to entirely turn around in the way one is thinking, believing, or living.* At this point, it's good to remember that you, too, have offended someone in the past and have stood in those very shoes of repentance.

The word "forgive" is the Greek word *aphiemi*, which means *to let it go, release,* or *to disregard.* It describes something *permanently dismissed.* Under these circumstances, we are required by God to dismiss the offense and let it go. In fact, it is permanently sent so far away, the right to ever bring it up again is forfeited. If the one who has offended us has sincerely asked for forgiveness, we are required to dismiss the offense and *never bring it up again.*

Seven Times a Day

Jesus continued His conversation about offense with the disciples saying, "And if he trespass against thee seven times in a day, and seven times in a day turn again to thee, saying, I repent; thou shalt forgive him" (Luke 17:4).

There are some people who don't intend to be offensive, but seem to continually say the wrong thing. With this type of person it is possible to be offended many times, even in a single day. Jesus instructed His disciples that if a person offends them seven times in a day and if that person repents every time, they must forgive them — *let it go and never bring it up again* — every time.

Do you know someone like this? Are you presented with the opportunity to forgive that person time and time again? The disciples knew exactly what Jesus was talking about. They were fully aware of how difficult it can be to forgive in the face of great offense. But still wanting to follow in their Master's footsteps, they asked Jesus for what they would need to accomplish this command — it is faith!

A Grain of a Mustard Seed

"And the apostles said unto the Lord, increase our faith" (Luke 17:5). And the Lord replied in Luke 17:6 saying, "...If ye had faith as a grain of mustard seed, ye might say unto this sycamine tree, Be thou plucked up by the root, and be thou planted in the sea; and it should obey you."

A grain of mustard seed is very small — the smallest seed in Israel. When the disciples imagined it would be difficult to do what Jesus was telling them to do, in essence they said, "Jesus, this is really tough. You're telling us to let go of the offense. Lord, increase our faith. We need more faith to do what You're saying." And Jesus responded to their request, "It really doesn't take much faith to do what I'm instructing you to do. You just need a little bit of faith — the size of a grain of a mustard seed. If you had just a little bit of faith, you could speak to a sycamine tree and it would obey."

Speak to the Sycamine Tree of Offense

Jesus compared offense to a sycamine tree. Why did Jesus choose a sycamine tree in this illustration? There are many types of trees in Israel and Jesus could have used any of them in speaking to His disciples, but he chose the sycamine tree.

Jesus definitely had a purpose in comparing offense to a sycamine tree, which often grew to heights of 35 feet. We will explore four specific reasons.

1. **The sycamine tree was the preferred wood for building caskets simply because it could grow anywhere.**

    The sycamine tree required very little water and could grow in very arid conditions. The wood of the sycamine tree was very durable, and therefore, often used for making caskets. By using the sycamine tree in this passage, Jesus indicated that *offense, bitterness, and unforgiveness* will "bury" the person carrying it.

2. **The sycamine tree had a very deep root system.**

    Cutting off a sycamine tree at the ground level did not kill this tree; it would simply regrow. To successfully remove the sycamine tree, it had to be completely uprooted. Jesus is saying the issue of offense and bitterness is rooted so deeply in the heart, it must be uprooted. As previously mentioned, *only repentance is able to uproot offense.*

3. **The sycamine tree looked very similar to the plum tree.**

    The fruit produced by plum trees was expensive and only the rich could afford to buy it. In contrast, the fruit from the sycamine tree was very inexpensive. The poor ate of the fruit of the sycamine tree because they couldn't afford the fruit of the plum tree. The fruit of the sycamine was very bitter and tart. In fact, it was so tart it wasn't uncommon for a hungry poor person to just nibble a little at a time because of its tartness. *The fruit of bitterness and offense will keep you spiritually poor if you eat of it.*

4. **The fruit of the sycamine tree was pollinated by the sting of a wasp.**

   The sycamine tree was the only known tree that was pollinated by the sting of a wasp. When people are offended or bitter, they will sometimes say, "I was really *stung* by someone." Often, they recount something that happened to them in the past where they were "stung" by the "wasp" of offense. *Offense is usually initiated when somebody feels "stung"* — offended by the words or actions of another person *or* the lack of words or actions by another.

If you are the one being described in this illustration — if you are being buried by thoughts that are hounding you, have offense deep within you, you are eating the bitter fruit of offense, or you have been "stung" by offense, what do you do?

The Answer To Dealing With Offense

Jesus provides the answer to dealing with offense in Luke 17:6: "If ye had faith as a grain of mustard seed, ye might say unto this sycamine tree, Be thou plucked up by the root, and be thou planted in the sea; and it should obey you."

Notice what Jesus says, "…Ye might *say* unto this sycamine tree…." You can *say* to the bitter offense that is burying and stinging you, "Be plucked up by the roots and be planted into the sea," and it *will* obey you."

Jesus did not say to "think about it" or "ponder it." He didn't even say "Pray about it." Jesus said you must SPEAK to it. If bitterness, unforgiveness, and offense are working in you, you must SPEAK — *speak* to the bitterness — *speak* to the unforgiveness — *speak* to the offense — *speak* to the "sycamine tree."

We must lift our voice, which represents the authority we have been given through Jesus Christ. Jesus instructs us that if we tell offense to "be plucked up by the roots and planted in the sea," it must obey the authority of our voice. We must be determined to pull out the roots of bitterness, unforgiveness, and offense. This does not merely provide temporary relief; it brings *permanent freedom!*

Planting Offense in the Sea

Why did Jesus say that we should tell offense to be "planted in the sea"? He said this because the sea is comprised of salt water, and salt water is so toxic to the sycamine tree it will kill it. If thrown into salt water, that plant will die and never grow back again.

In this passage, Jesus is not suggesting we temporarily rid ourselves of offense. He is talking about *permanent deliverance of offense* from our heart, so that offense dies and never takes root again.

Offense Must Obey

And finally, Jesus reminds the disciples, and us, "…and it [the offense] should *obey* you" (Luke 17:6). The meaning of the word "obey" in this verse is *to fall in line*. We can *listen* to offense and to our emotions and allow them to control us or we can *speak* to them. When we use our voice with the authority God gave us, those offenses must *fall in line* — they must obey what we tell them to do — to be cut off at the root and cast into the sea.

It's time for you to begin to lift your voice. If you will speak to your emotions, they will obey. If you will speak to offense, it must obey. You can be set completely free from the control of offense if you will simply SPEAK to it. *Offense will obey and you will walk free!*

STUDY QUESTIONS

Study to shew thyself approved unto God, a workman that needeth not to be ashamed, rightly dividing the word of truth.
— 2 Timothy 2:15

1. How does unforgiveness hinder the will of God for your life? How many times did Jesus tell us we must forgive in one day? Read Ephesians 4:32. What does it say about forgiving others?

2. Describe the effects of allowing offense to take root in your heart. What is the resulting fruit and how does it affect those around you?

PRACTICAL APPLICATION

> But be ye doers of the word, and not hearers only,
> deceiving your own selves.
> —James 1:22

1. What are the only two ways we can receive offense in our lives? Think back over your life as a Christian. Can you remember a time when you took offense? Which of the two categories for receiving offense did it fall into? How did you get free from it?

2. Examine your heart. If you find any offense, what steps will you take to permanently walk free of it?

Notes

_____

_____

_____

_____

_____

_____

_____

_____

_____

_____

_____

_____

_____

_____

_____

_____

_____

_____

_____

_____

_____

_____

_____

_____

_____

_____

_____

_____

Notes

www.ingramcontent.com/pod-product-compliance
Lightning Source LLC
Chambersburg PA
CBHW071802020426
42331CB00008B/2370